Word 365
Track Changes

EASY WORD 365 ESSENTIALS - BOOK 6

M.L. HUMPHREY

SELECT TITLES BY M.L. HUMPHREY

WORD 365 ESSENTIALS
Word 365 for Beginners
Intermediate Word 365

EASY WORD 365 ESSENTIALS
Text Formatting
Page Formatting
Lists
Tables
Styles and Breaks
Track Changes

See mlhumphrey.com for more Microsoft Office titles

CONTENTS

Introduction

This book is part of the *Easy Word 365 Essentials* series of titles. These are targeted titles that are excerpted from the main *Word 365 Essentials* series and are focused on one specific topic.

If you want a more general introduction to Word, then you should check out the *Word 365 Essentials* titles instead. In this case, *Intermediate Word 365* which covers not only track changes but styles, breaks, multilevel lists, tables, and more.

But if all you want to learn is how to use track changes in Word, then this is the book for you.

Track Changes

Now we are up to track changes, which are amazing and wonderful and made my corporate life much, much easier.

When I first started we had a few people in my office who would manually format text to show changes. Which meant that you had to manually reformat that text to finalize the document. It was a nightmare.

With track changes, someone can make edits to your document and you can see those edits but then all you have to do is accept or reject those changes and they're incorporated into your document and you're done. It's fantastic.

Also, you can navigate through your document one change at a time so that you don't miss anything. No stray comma or period that gets skipped over because it's such a small change.

But you have to be careful with track changes. Some of the views that Word now offers with respect to track changes don't show them. So you can miss that there are track changes in a document and send it off to an outside party and they open it up and they see all of those little changes and who made them. Not a good thing.

If you use track changes, you have to be careful to accept all changes and turn them off when you're done.

Okay. Let's tackle this topic. I'm going to save comments, which go hand-in-hand with track changes, for the next chapter.

When you open a document that has track changes turned on, Word will now (as of January 2023 in Word 365) give you a warning message that track changes are on:

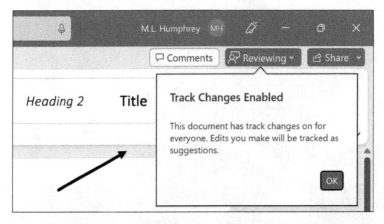

This is a good thing. You never want to work in a document that has track changes turned on without realizing you are doing so.

First things first.

Turn On or Off Track Changes

To turn on or off track changes you can use Ctrl + Shift + E. There is also an option to do so in the Tracking section of the Review tab:

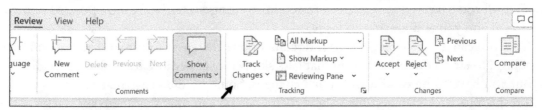

To turn on track changes, just click on that image that says Track Changes. To turn it off, click on it again. You want to click onto the image part of that option, not the text part. And you don't need the dropdown. So aim for the pen or pencil or whatever that is.

And I want to make a point here. It is possible to have a document that shows track changes, but that also has other changes that were made to the document that are not visible because someone temporarily turned off track changes and then made edits. So if it is really, really important that you see every single change in a document, use Document Compare to see all edits instead of trusting that track changes captured everything.

(Usually this is not some nefarious deliberate thing that happens. In past versions of Word I would turn off track changes when making formatting or non-essential changes to tables because the way Word showed track changes for tables was ugly and confusing and didn't really let people see what it would look like when final and most users don't want to see every little formatting change. But sometimes I'd also forget to turn it back on.)

Okay. So. Turn on track changes and make your edits.

Appearance

Here is an example of track changes with two different users:

> This is a sample document that I'm creating on my other computer to see if I can show you track changes made by ~~two~~ different users. It may or may not work because both of these computers are tied into the same Microsoft account. But let's give it a go.
>
> I have now turned T̶track ̶eChanges on in my document and you can see that any new text I add is underlined and colored a different color.
>
> This is me working on this same document on a different computer. I stripped out the Author information before I saved this version of this document so that I could appear as two different users.

Text additions that are recorded by Track Changes are underlined and color-coded. Deletions have a strikethrough and are also color-coded but are not underlined.

Above you can see that "two" in that first paragraph was deleted. And that the second and third paragraphs were all text that was added after Track Changes was turned on. The second paragraph is blue, the third is red, to indicate different users.

(For those of you reading in black and white, you won't be able to see the colors that distinguish the different users, but should still be able to see the additions and deletions.)

Also, you can see that in the second paragraph the first user wrote "track changes" and the second user changed that to "Track Changes".

For each tracked change, on the left-hand side of the text there is a vertical black line indicating that a change was made at that location.

Word automatically assigns colors to users and this can change, so you can't assume that a user will always be assigned the same color each time. The color assigned to a specific user will always be consistent within a document while that document remains open, but the color assigned to a user can change when the document is reopened

For example, when I wrote that first paragraph on my old laptop the changes were in red. But when I opened that document on my new laptop the changes were in blue. So you need to check each time when you review a document which user is assigned to which color.

Users

All changes made when Track Changes are turned on are assigned to users. By default, each user is assigned their own color. This is normally based upon the associated Microsoft Office account of the user, not the computer.

So, for example, when I worked on a document on one computer and then transferred it to another, my changes on the new computer were given the same color because both computers are tied into my Microsoft Office account. (I was able to get the two colors you can see in the example above only when I stripped the author information from the document after I made the first set of edits.)

To see who the user is for a specific edit, you have a couple options.

The first option is to hold your mouse over the edit:

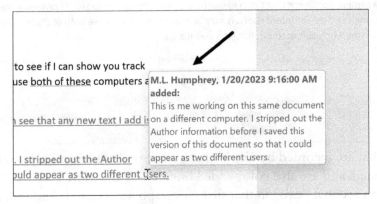

Note that also shows the time and date when the edit was made.

The second option is to show the Reviewing Pane.

Reviewing Pane

The Reviewing Pane can be turned on or off using the Reviewing Pane dropdown menu in the Tracking section of the Review tab:

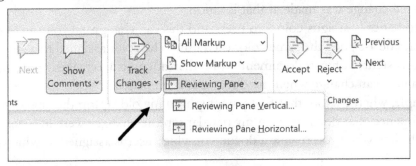

You have the choice of a vertical pane or a horizontal pane. My preference is for the vertical pane, although usually I don't actually use a reviewing pane at all:

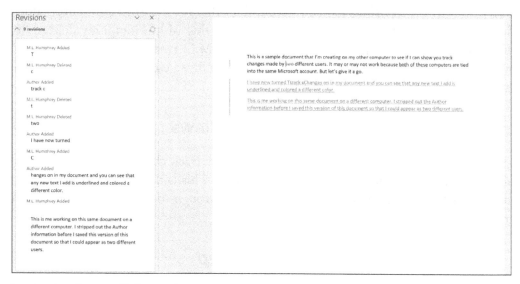

The Reviewing Pane will list each revision in the document as well as who made that revision. So you can see here that the two users that Word is tracking are Author and M.L. Humphrey.

The reason I'm not a huge fan of using it for simple track changes is because it's much easier for me to see what's happening in the document itself than to interpret that list of revisions.

For example, here:

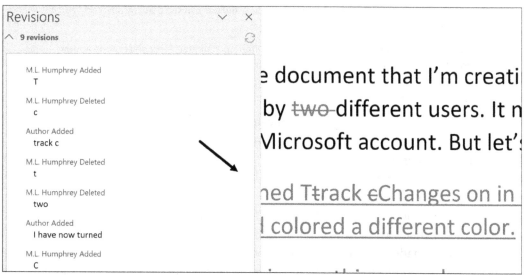

It's pretty easy looking at the text to see that one user wrote the words "track changes" and that another user came along and capitalized them so that it became "Track Changes".

But if I look in the Revisions panel, I have listings that tell me M.L. Humphrey added "T" and deleted "c" and that Author added "track c" and that M.L. Humphrey deleted "t" and then it lists two unrelated edits and finally tells me that M.L. Humphrey added "C".

The list of revisions is accurate, but reading through those edits one at a time is confusing. So I don't do it usually.

Track Changes Views

I personally like this view that's the default view for my track changes, All Markup. It shows me the old text as well as all edits that have been made. This is the view I try to keep active at all times unless I need a different view. But let's walk through those other choices in case you need them.

Simple Markup

This is the Simple Markup view:

> This is a sample document that I'm creating on my other computer to see if I can show you track changes made by different users. It may or may not work because both of these computers are tied into the same Microsoft account. But let's give it a go.
>
> I have now turned Track Changes on in my document and you can see that any new text I add is underlined and colored a different color.
>
> This is me working on this same document on a different computer. I stripped out the Author information before I saved this version of this document so that I could appear as two different users.

It has a red vertical line off to the side to indicate where edits have been made, but, other than that, it's the final document with all changes made.

It's good for seeing what the final product will look like. So a good last-pass option. It makes sure that you catch any extra spaces or double periods or things like that that can slip through when track changes are on.

But for me it is not a good working option. Many times I found as I was working with teams on projects that I really did need to know what was originally written, how that was changed, and who made the change. Hate to say it, but if the lawyer with twenty years of experience made the edit to that technical paragraph that was written by the brand new analyst I'm more likely to trust that edit was correct than if the brand new analyst edited something written by the lawyer. Context often matters.

No Markup

This is the No Markup view:

> This is a sample document that I'm creating on my other computer to see if I can show you track changes made by different users. It may or may not work because both of these computers are tied into the same Microsoft account. But let's give it a go.
>
> I have now turned Track Changes on in my document and you can see that any new text I add is underlined and colored a different color.
>
> This is me working on this same document on a different computer. I stripped out the Author information before I saved this version of this document so that I could appear as two different users.

It has no indication that there are any track changes in the document. The text reflects all of the changes that were made. But there is no way to see that track changes is on.

I would use this one only if I were printing off a copy of the document for review by a senior person who needed to review the "final" but where I wasn't yet willing to remove tracked changes yet. It would allow printing of a completely clean copy and wouldn't distract that senior person with notations of where changes had been made.

But I'd immediately get away from this view as soon as I printed the document. I would never leave a document in this view.

(As someone whose job used to be investigating financial institutions for rule violations that sometimes carried hefty fines, trust me that you don't want to forget that a document has track changes still visible.)

Original

This is the Original view:

> This is a sample document that I'm creating on my other computer to see if I can show you track changes made by two different users. It may or may not work because both of these computers are tied into the same Microsoft account. But let's give it a go.

This is another one I would never, ever leave my document in for any length of time. But sometimes it can be helpful to look at the document as it existed prior to any edits. Especially when there are multiple users making edits to the same text. That lets you see what the source text really was.

All Markup

And then finally, as a reminder, this is the All Markup view:

> This is a sample document that I'm creating on my other computer to see if I can show you track changes made by ~~two~~ different users. It may or may not work because both of these computers are tied into the same Microsoft account. But let's give it a go.
>
> I have now turned Ttrack eChanges on in my document and you can see that any new text I add is underlined and colored a different color.
>
> This is me working on this same document on a different computer. I stripped out the Author information before I saved this version of this document so that I could appear as two different users.

It shows the original text in black and then marks the location of any changes with a black vertical line off to the side of the text. All additions and deletions in the document are shown with colored text. For me, this is the best one to see what was done to the original text and whether I agree.

A Quick Warning

If it matters to you who made what changes in your document, then never ever do what I did above to give you these examples. I achieved that effect by stripping out the Author information from the document. And right now that All Markup example looks great. It has changes by two distinct users and we can see what each of them did. But as soon as I save changes to that document, all of the changes will be assigned to Author.

I had this happen on a big project. Some analyst stripped out the author information from the original document and then circulated it to a team of six for edits. And no one noticed what was happening until we had a final document where all edits appeared as if they'd been made by one user. It was horrible.

So if you must strip out the author information from a document, save a copy of that document as it existed right before you do that and then strip those properties out of your document only when the document is final and ready to be distributed. Never strip author information from a document that is still a work in progress that may require the use of track changes.

Show Markup Options

One final basic appearance setting that we have not yet covered is the Show Markup dropdown menu available in the Tracking section of the Review tab:

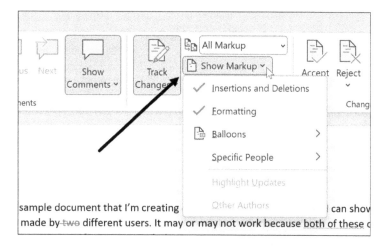

By default, Word will show both insertions/deletions and formatting changes. Here is an example with formatting changes included:

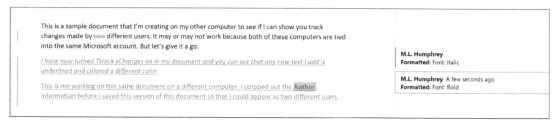

There are times when you really don't need to see all the formatting changes. I am a control freak so I always wanted to see them, but for a lawyer whose focus is on the words and the commas, they don't need to see that you reformatted the headers throughout the document.

So if you don't want to see the formatting changes listed out, click on that option to turn it off. Or if you do want to see them and they're off, click on that option to turn it on.

You can also choose how changes in the document are shown. By default, only formatting changes are shown in "balloons" which are the notes off to the side, but you can actually choose to show all revisions that way or to show all revisions inline in the document:

Here is an example that shows revisions in balloons:

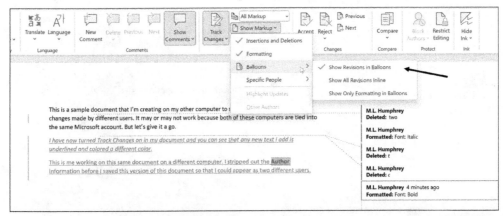

The nice thing about this setting is that it takes out deleted text from your document so you still can see changes in the document but you don't have to mentally remove the deleted text. See the Track Changes example there in the second paragraph as an example of how that works.

Show revisions inline basically is what you saw above with the All Markup screenshot, but this time there's no note off to the side to call-out the formatting changes. They're just there with no specific mention that they were made. (So not a setting I personally like to use.)

Finally, you can choose to only see edits from specific people if you want. Again, personally, not something I would do because I was always looking at the entirety of the document and whether the entire thing worked as a final report. But I'm sure there are times when it makes sense to hide the edits made by one specific user. For example, maybe if an analyst reformatted the document with track changes on and you don't want those changes flagged during your review.

Advanced Options

You can customize track changes by clicking on the expansion arrow in the Tracking section of the Review tab to open the Track Changes Options dialogue box:

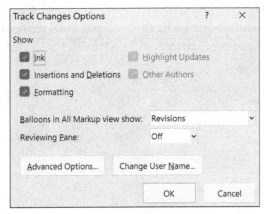

That allows you to then click on Advanced Options to open the Advanced Track Changes Options dialogue box:

This is where you can change the colors used for tracking changes as well as how tracked changes are shown in the document. So you could set it so that there is just one color used for all changes regardless of the author and you could even choose what that color is.

I want to say back in the day legal documents used a double black-line strikethrough for deletions, for example. This is where you could set your document to do that.

Just know that this is a personal setting that will apply for your version of the document, but not for someone else looking at the same document.

Okay, now that we've covered all of the appearance settings, time to actually review the changes and accept them or reject them.

Review Changes

To review the changes in your document, you can turn on the Reviewing Pane and scroll through that way, but what I prefer is to either read the document or, if there are scattered or small changes, use the Previous and Next options in the Changes section of the Review tab:

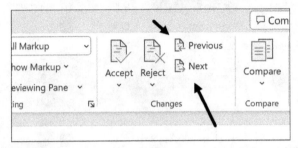

Click on Next to move forward to the next change in the document. Word will move through the document, find the next change, and highlight it. Click on Previous to move backward through the document.

Accept or Reject Changes

In that same section, you have the option to Accept or Reject. Both of those have a dropdown menu with a variety of choices.

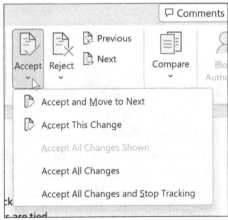

Here you can see that for Accept the options are to accept and move to next, accept this change, accept all changes, or accept all changes and stop tracking.

I tend not to accept or reject a single change at a time. And the reason for that is what you can see with that track changes edit. Word considers that six separate changes. First was the addition of track and changes, then was the deletion of the lower-case t and c, and then was the addition of the upper-case t and c.

Rather than walk through those six changes and accept them individually, what I do is select both words and then click on Accept. That accepts all six changes at once.

So usually I walk through a document using previous and next, read that phrase, sentence, or paragraph, make any additional edits I think are needed and then select the whole thing and accept the edits. (Assuming this is a final pass that no one else needs to review. Obviously, don't accept all changes if someone needs to see what you did.)

Turn Off Track Changes

When you are done with your document and all changes have been made and accepted, turn off track changes. Yes, I have said this ten times. I probably need to say it ten more. DO NOT leave track changes turned on in your document. One, it's a nuisance if you then go to make any edit whatsoever to the document. And, two, you do not want to run the risk of circulating a "final" document that actually has a bunch of tracked changes in it.

When track changes is on, your status in the top right corner will be Reviewing and when it is off your status will be Editing.

Final Document Review

Before you finalize your document, you can have Word review the document for any lingering tracked changes that weren't accepted or rejected.

To do so, go to the File tab and then click on Info. There is an option there to Inspect Document. Click on Check for Issues to see if there are still tracked changes present in the document:

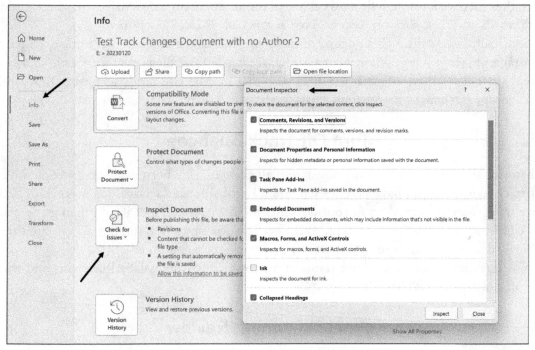

It will be part of the Comments, Revisions, and Versions option.

(Just be careful about removing your document properties and personal information, which I warned about above. That is under Document Properties and Personal Information.)

Comments

For me, comments in Word go hand-in-hand with track changes, but they're actually two separate things, so I've separated them into two separate chapters. Here is an example of a comment and the beginning of a response:

You can see that by default comments are visible off to the side of the main text and that the document will have a little comment bubble there to the right of the text to indicate the existence of a comment.

I left the response unfinished so you could also see that tip that says to use Ctrl + Enter to post a response. If you just use Enter, it goes to a new line within the comment. Your other option for finalizing a comment is to click on that blue button with the arrow in it.

Here is what it looks like when someone has made a comment and then someone else has responded to that comment:

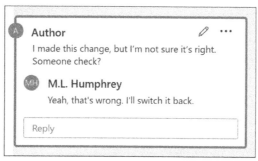

To edit a response, just hold your cursor over it and you'll see the pencil appear next to the name of the person who commented. Click on that and then make your changes.

One fault in Word is that you can actually edit someone else's comment. So I can click on that little pencil in the top right corner of the comment box and edit the comment made by Author even though I'm currently M.L. Humphrey to Word.

Alright. So how do you add a comment in the first place?

Place your cursor at the location in the document where you want to make a comment and then go to the Comments section of the Review tab and click on New Comment:

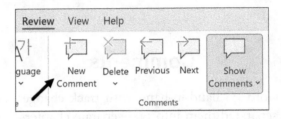

You can also use Ctrl + Alt + M or right-click and choose New Comment from the dropdown menu. When you click on that option, Word will insert a new comment window with the cursor in the beginning of the comment window. You can either type your text and then use Ctrl + Enter or the button with the blue arrow to add that comment or click on the X if you changed your mind.

While a comment is selected, Word shifts it to the left like you can see below with the middle comment.

When no comments are selected they all align.

The Delete option in the Comments section will let you delete the current comment, delete all comments in the document, or delete all resolved comments. You can also click on an individual comment and then right-click on the … in the top right corner and choose Delete Thread to delete a comment and any responses.

To Resolve a comment, right-click on the … in the top right corner of the comment and then choose to Resolve Thread:

The comment will be marked as Resolved and grayed out, but will still appear in your document:

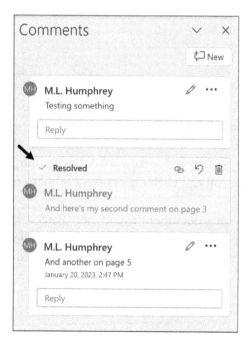

This option is not available if you are in Compatibility Mode, so have opened a .doc file instead of a .docx file.

The Show Comments dropdown in the Comments section has two options, Contextual or List. Contextual places the comments next to where they were made in the document. List shows all comments from the document in a Comments task pane:

The comments are all listed together regardless of what page they appear on. Above, for example, there were comments I made on page 1, page 3, and page 5. Even when I scroll to page 7, all three of those comments are listed in that task pane. Whereas with the Contextual option they only show when you're on the page where the comment was made.

If you are in the List view, you can click on a comment to go to the page that contains that comment.

You can make comments on a document even when Track Changes are turned off.

If you have track changes in a document that display in a balloon off to the right side, any comments will be pushed to the right of those tracked changes and may not be readily visible.

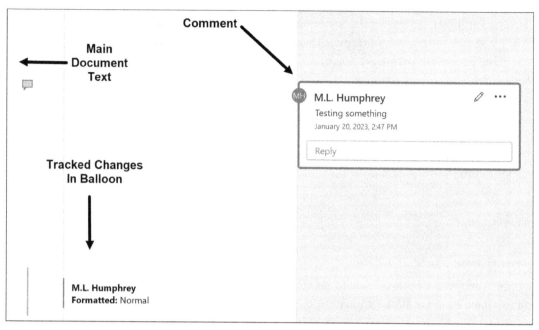

You can fix this by setting tracked changes to display inline.

Another option is to click on the Comments button in the top right corner of the workspace to open the Comments task pane to see the text of your comments, but that task pane will appear on top of any tracked changes balloons. If you close the Navigation task pane, however, then you can have the Comments task pane visible as well as any tracked changes shown in balloons.

You can use the Previous and Next options in the Comments section of the Review tab to move through the comments in your document.

However, Word will skip any comments that have been marked as resolved. Furthermore, it will not show those comments off to the side with your active comments. They will only be indicated by the comment icon to the right of your text.

Here is one open comment with the comment displayed and then you can see the comment bubble for a resolve comment below that:

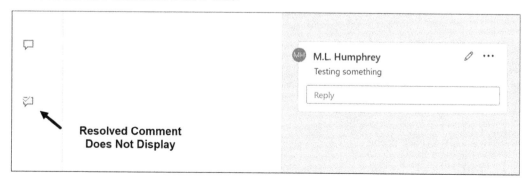

You can still see the resolved comment by clicking on that comment bubble.

Also, you cannot make a comment directly on a footnote or endnote. (That would be very nice to have Microsoft people, if you're looking for things you can do to improve the program.)

If you're used to how comments worked previously in Word, including with a dotted line between the comment and text it was addressing, you can currently revert back to the old way of doing things by going to the File tab and then Options and the General page and unchecking the box for Enable Modern Comments.

Here's how that used to look with a dotted line between the comment and where in the document someone was trying to place that comment:

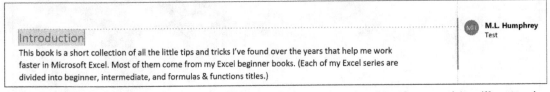

They are going to retire the ability to switch back at some point, but for now it's still an option. You may have to close Word and reopen before that change takes effect, though.

Compare Documents

The final aspect to track changes and comments is comparing documents. I mentioned it before, because it's the most sure-fire way to know that you're seeing all changes that were made to a document. You take the original document, you take the new document, and you give them both to Word and tell it to flag any changes.

But it can also be a bit messy at times especially if text was moved around. Still, it's nice to know about if you need it.

First step, open a new document in Word. Go to the Review tab and find the Compare dropdown in the Compare section on the right-hand side. Click on Compare.

The Compare Documents dialogue box will appear:

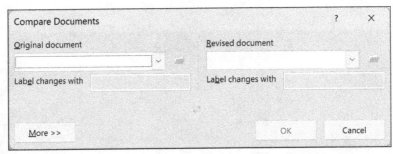

The left-hand side is the original of the document. The right-hand side is the updated version. Click on the dropdown menu to see recent documents you've used and select one of those files or use the little folder to the right of the dropdown to go find your file.

Word will automatically populate the Label Changes With field with a user name, but you can change that if you want.

Click on More to tell Word which changes to identify and how to treat changes like the one we talked about before with "track changes" being changed to "Track Changes".

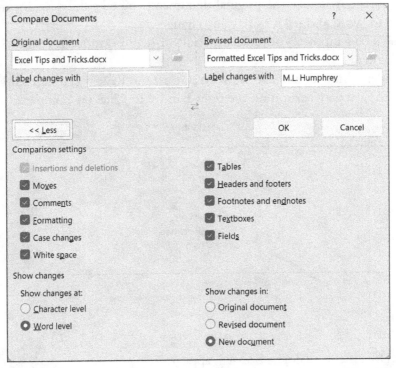

If you choose to show changes at the character level then it will look like the example from above. If you choose to show at the word level it will show that as a deletion of track changes replaced with an insertion of Track Changes instead of just changes to the individual letters.

You can also choose whether to show those changes in the original document, the revised document, or a new document. The default is new document which is what I always choose as well.

Click on OK when you're done. Here we go:

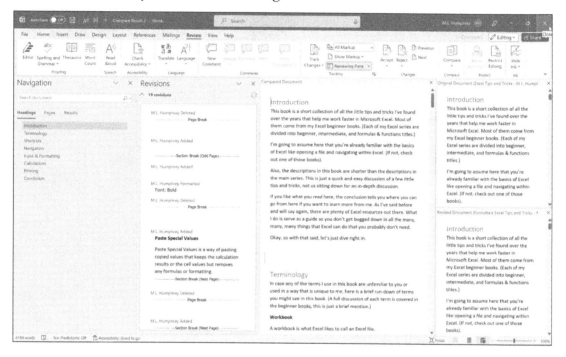

That looks chaotic, but we can hide the Navigation pane and that leaves me with a Revisions pane on the left-hand side, the new document in the center and then the original document on the top right and the revised document on the bottom right.

Click on an edit in the Revisions pane to go to that section of the other documents:

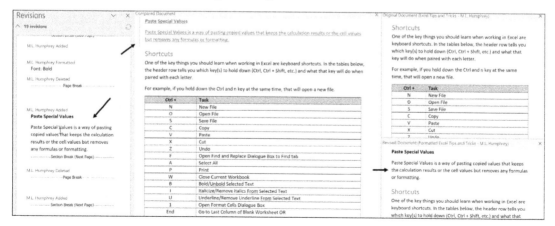

You can see above, for example, a change I made where I added text related to Paste Special Values within the document. Word recorded that as adding text. You can see it reflected as a tracked change in the new document, see that that text was not in the original, and see that text in the revised document.

I often find with document compare that I just want to view the new comparison document. You can do that by clicking on the X in the corner of the original and revised documents to close them.

That also makes the page breaks in the new comparison document appear, which helps me understand what this particular change was:

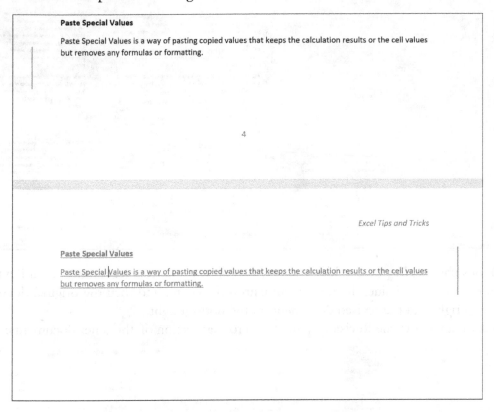

Now I can see (and remember) that what I did here was copy text from the end of that chapter and paste it in there so that I would force the chapter start to the next page. I did that so I could demonstrate a specific type of section break. The fact that the text was not part of the next chapter was not obvious if you look at the screenshot above this one because Word in that view was not showing page and section breaks on the screen.

But you can see that what I ended up with was a document that has track changes that reflect formatting changes, the addition/deletion of page and section breaks, and the addition of headers and footers as well.

Usually I only need this when a document was edited but not in track changes. I have also used it when someone edited a document and some of the changes I made to their edits were to reject additions or deletions they made, which you can't see in track changes at the end.

So what I did in that situation is accepted all changes in their version and then compared that document to my final version after I had accepted or rejected their changes. That left me with a document where the only track changes in the document were edits on their edits.

Appendix A: Basic Terminology Recap

These terms were covered in detail in *Word 365 for Beginners*. This is just meant as a refresher.

Tab

When I refer to a tab, I am referring to the menu options at the top of the screen. The tab options that are available by default are File, Home, Insert, Draw, Design, Layout, References, Mailings, Review, View, and Help, but for certain tasks additional tabs will appear.

Click

If I tell you to click on something, that means to move your cursor over to that location and then either right-click or left-click. If I don't say which to do, left-click.

Left-Click / Right-Click

A left-click is generally for selecting something and involves using the left-hand side of your mouse or bottom left-hand corner of your trackpad. A right-click is generally for opening a dropdown menu and involves using the right-hand side of your mouse or bottom right-hand corner of your trackpad.

Left-Click and Drag

Left-click and drag means to left-click and then hold that left-click as you move your mouse.

Dropdown Menu

A dropdown menu is a list of choices that you can view by right-clicking in a specific spot or clicking on an arrow next to or below one of the available choices under the tabs up top. Depending on where you are in the workspace, a dropdown menu may actually drop upward from that spot.

Expansion Arrow

In the bottom right corner of some of the sections under the tabs in the top menu you will see an arrow, which I refer to as an expansion arrow. Clicking on an expansion arrow will usually open a dialogue box or task pane and is often the way to see the largest number of options.

Dialogue Box

A dialogue box is a pop-up box that will open on top of your workspace and will usually include the largest number of choices for that particular setting or task.

Scroll Bar

Scroll bars appear when there are more options than can appear on the screen or when your document is longer than will show on the screen. They can be used to move through the remainder of the choices or document.

Task Pane

A task pane is a set of additional options that will appear to the sides or even below the main workspace. The Navigation pane is by default visible on the left-hand side of the workspace. You can close a task pane by clicking on the X in the top right corner of the pane.

Control Shortcuts

Control shortcuts are shortcuts that let you perform certain tasks in Word. I will write them as Ctrl + and then a character. That means to hold down both the Ctrl key and that character. So Ctrl + C means hold down Ctrl and C, which will let you copy your selection. Even though I will write each shortcut using a capital letter it doesn't have to be the capitalized version to work.

About the Author

M.L. Humphrey is a former stockbroker with a degree in Economics from Stanford and an MBA from Wharton who has spent close to twenty years as a regulator and consultant in the financial services industry.

You can reach M.L. at mlhumphreywriter@gmail.com or at mlhumphrey.com.

www.ingramcontent.com/pod-product-compliance
Lightning Source LLC
Chambersburg PA
CBHW060512060326
40689CB00020B/4715